THE ULTIMATE BABY-SITTER'S HANDBOOK

(So You Wanna Make Tons of Money?)

Written by
Debra Mostow Zakarin

Illustrated by
Ruta Daugavietis

Designed by
Kristin Lock

PSS!
PRICE STERN SLOAN

Library of Congress Catalog Card Number: 96-42997
ISBN: 0-8431-7936-8

Zakarin, Debra Mostow.

The ultimate baby-sitter's handbook: So you wanna make tons of money? / by Debra Mostow
Zakarin ; illustrated by Ruta Daugavietis.

p.   cm.

Summary: A guide to baby-sitting, providing tips on how to get started and how to deal with
challenging situations.

ISBN 0-8431-7936-8

1. Babysitting—Handbooks, manuals, etc.—Juvenile literature.

2. Babysitters—Handbooks, manuals, etc.—Juvenile literature.

3. Money-making projects for children—Juvenile literature.

[1. Babysitting—Handbooks, manuals, etc. 2. Babysitters—Handbooks, manuals, etc.]

I. Daugavietis, Ruta, ill. II. Title.

HQ769.5.Z35   1997

649'.1'0248—dc20   96-42997

                                              CIP

                                              AC

Visit us online at our cool Website:
http://www.penguinputnam.com/yreaders/index.htm

13 15 17 19 20 18 16 14 12

PSS! ® is a registered trademark of Price Stern Sloan, Inc.
Plugged In™ is a trademark of Price Stern Sloan, Inc.

For my favorite sister,
Sari, the true instigator behind all of
our baby-sitting antics.

TABLE OF CONTENTS

INTRODUCTION

My older sister and I weren't very particular about the *type* of baby-sitter we wanted. Our only request was that she have long hair so that we could play beauty parlor and make–believe she was our client while we were the beauticians.

Mostly we behaved with our baby-sitter, but not always. One night, after our baby-sitter tucked us into bed and said goodnight, my sister and I sneaked out of

bed and proceeded to stuff wads of paper towels down the toilet. Could you believe that the toilet began to overflow? Our parents came home to the baby-sitter and our next-door neighbor wearing rain boots and wading knee deep in water—inside the  house. They were not amused. And our poor baby-sitter never managed to make it back!

But that incident taught me a lesson I remembered when I grew up and began baby-sitting myself. I made sure to check on the kids every fifteen minutes or so—especially if the kids were quiet. Lack of noise is, as a rule, a sign that mischievous behavior is *definitely* going on. I wasn't going to take any chances!

And the more I did it, the more I loved baby-sitting. Playing with and taking care of children was very fun not to mention a great way to make some bucks! The more experienced I became as a baby-sitter, and the better prepared I was, the more I actually enjoyed myself. Surprise! So that's why I decided to write this book and share some of my best-kept secrets with you. Because the biggest secret of all is that baby-sitting is a great way to have fun, gain valuable job experience, and earn the money to do all the cool things you wouldn't get to do otherwise.

The hardest part about baby-sitting is getting started. Kids to Watch (or KTWs, as I call the kids you will baby-sit) are both fun and sometimes complicated. This book is intended to teach you how to start your baby-sitting business, get organized, be the best baby-sitter you can possibly be—and make money, too! Also included throughout are stories and anecdotes from other baby-sitters, which I'm sure you'll enjoy!

Happy Baby-sitting!

CHAPTER 1

HOW TO START YOUR OWN SUCCESSFUL BABY-SITTING BUSINESS

OK, you've decided you want to baby-sit because it's a great way to earn money and because it's fun! But like many fun activities such as playing video games and bungee jumping, baby-sitting isn't for everyone. How do you find out if you're one of the chosen few?

Before you get started, ask yourself these questions:

1. Is it OK with your parents or guardians? YES □ NO □

2. Do you like kids? YES □ NO □

3. Will baby-sitting interfere with your schoolwork or other extracurricular activities? YES □ NO □

4. Are you very responsible? YES □ NO □

5. Do you have the time and energy to baby-sit? YES □ NO □

If you've answered yes to all, or at least four, of the above questions, then you are ready for the job at hand. Let's get started!

Finding Clients Safely

Word of Mouth

One of the best ways to advertise is by word of mouth. This is how it works: Tell everyone you know that you are ready, willing, and able to begin baby-sitting immediately. This includes telling your friends, relatives, your

parents' friends, neighbors, teachers, school secretaries . . . in other words, EVERYONE!

Once you tell one person, they'll tell another person, who will tell one more person. You get the idea. It goes on and on. . . . This is one time when having a big mouth can actually help you!

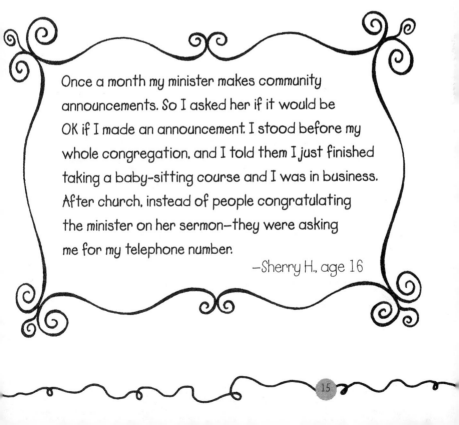

Once a month my minister makes community announcements. So I asked her if it would be OK if I made an announcement. I stood before my whole congregation, and I told them I just finished taking a baby-sitting course and I was in business. After church, instead of people congratulating the minister on her sermon—they were asking me for my telephone number.

—Sherry H., age 16

Advertising

Advertising is another efficient way of getting the word out. Hang flyers on bulletin boards at your church, synagogue, local YMCA, boys' and girls' clubs, and country club. Always make sure to get permission first from whomever is in charge of postings for the bulletin board.

Your baby-sitting flyer needs to include your name, telephone number, age, and when you are available to baby-sit. Remember to be neat, clear, and professional because this flyer could be the first impression for many new and potential clients. Your flyer doesn't have to be fancy. Simple and clear is a safe bet. And you don't have to hand write each flyer. Most local copy centers charge between one to two cents per copy.

ADVERTISING SAFETY

Advertising Safety: Accepting jobs from strangers is not as safe as baby-sitting for a neighbor or a neighbor's friend. Get to know your employer. You can even ask them for references. Your safety should always be your #1 concern.

RESPONSIBLE BABY-SITTER

- FRIENDLY
- EXPERIENCED
- COMPETITIVE FEES
- AVAILABLE:
  - (WEEKDAY EVENINGS
  - WEEKEND DAYS & EVENINGS
- REFERENCES AVAILABLE

FOR MORE INFORMATION, PLEASE CALL...

DEBRA @ (555) 555-1212

AFTER 6:00 P.M. OR PLEASE LEAVE A MESSAGE

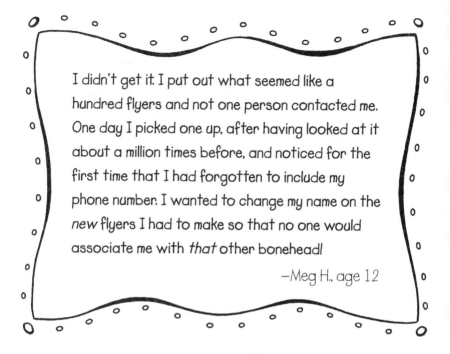

I didn't get it. I put out what seemed like a hundred flyers and not one person contacted me. One day I picked one up, after having looked at it about a million times before, and noticed for the first time that I had forgotten to include my phone number. I wanted to change my name on the *new* flyers I had to make so that no one would associate me with *that* other bonehead!

—Meg H., age 12

Mailing Flyers

In addition to spreading the word to all your friends, relatives, neighbors, and parents' friends, why not mail or drop

off a flyer in their mailboxes announcing that you are in the baby-sitting business? The flyer you use to advertise on local bulletin boards can be the same flyer sent out to people you know. Try to deliver the flyers yourself during the daytime on weekends or after school in order to save money on postage and to catch potential clients when they are home. Using brightly colored paper will make your flyer stand out. Or, if you do decide to do a mailing, send colored postcards. Postcards will help reduce your postage costs. There is no need to buy fancy postcards. Buy a packet of brightly colored index cards and put all the baby-sitting information on one side and the person's address to whom you are mailing it on the other side.

Business Cards

Business cards are another effective means of advertising. You can make your own business cards out of colored index cards, even cutting slits in them at the bottom so they fit in a standard business card file or Rolodex™. If you happen to have extra money to invest, you can order business cards from a local copy center or stationery store. Business cards can also be posted on bulletin boards, mailed out, and left at the homes of your clients for easy reference in the future. When posting business cards on bulletin boards, leave a few so that potential clients may take them home. A business card should also be clear and simple.

Baby-sitting Classes and First-Aid Courses

Many local YMCAs, community centers, the American Red Cross, and even some hospitals offer courses in baby-sitting. This is *definitely* a class a first-time, and even a more experienced baby-sitter should take before beginning work.  Not only will you learn valuable information to make you the best, but this is also a great place to *network*, which means spreading the word to others to let them know that you are in business.

If you take a baby-sitting class or a first-aid course, don't forget to include this information on your flyer or business card. This is the kind of stuff potential clients are interested in knowing. And, of course, don't forget to include your name or telephone number. If you can't remember simple tasks like these, potential clients will be very frightened that you may forget something crucial while baby-sitting their children. Remember, every contact you have with a potential client will leave an impression—whether it's positive or negative depends largely on you!

How Much Money?

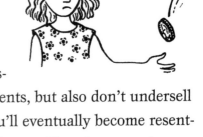

Deciding how much to charge can be a difficult decision-making process. Remember, you are a profes-sional. Don't overcharge clients, but also don't undersell your services. If you do, you'll eventually become resent-ful toward your clients, and you will no longer enjoy taking jobs. Even though making money is one of the rea-sons for going into business, remember that it is just one aspect of babysitting. Don't let it overshadow the fun!

Baby-sitters usually charge an hourly rate and are paid in cash the day or evening the job has ended. If you have a steady job working for the same client every day or every other day after school, you may want to make alter-nate payment arrangements.
It may be easier for the client to pay you once a week. Cash is always the easiest form of

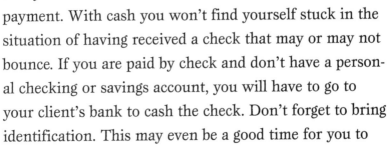

payment. With cash you won't find yourself stuck in the situation of having received a check that may or may not bounce. If you are paid by check and don't have a person-al checking or savings account, you will have to go to your client's bank to cash the check. Don't forget to bring identification. This may even be a good time for you to

open up your own account at the bank. Remember, the custom of hiding your money under your mattress went out of style in your great-grandmother's day!

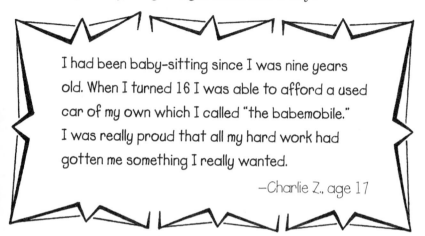

I had been baby-sitting since I was nine years old. When I turned 16 I was able to afford a used car of my own which I called "the babemobile." I was really proud that all my hard work had gotten me something I really wanted.

—Charlie Z., age 17

Ask other baby-sitters in your neighborhood what the approximate hourly rate in your area is. Try asking a neighbor whom you know has kids what they normally pay a baby-sitter and what they believe is a fair price. Use all of this information to determine your baby-sitting rate.

The following are times when it is appropriate and makes sense to raise your rates:

- After midnight charge 50¢ more per hour;

- charge extra for three or more children; either charge extra per child or add a set amount to the total;

- charge extra per hour for holidays; some baby-sitters even double their usual rate on New Year's Eve.

DEBRA'S
RATE CARD

DAY/EVENING RATE:
$ (fill in your rate) per hour

AFTER MIDNIGHT:
$ (fill in your rate) per hour
PLUS 50¢ extra per hour after midnight

3 OR MORE CHILDREN:
$ (rate) per hour PLUS $2.00 extra per child

HOLIDAY RATE:
$ (fill in your rate) per hour PLUS 50¢ extra
per hour after midnight

DEBRA

Most importantly, make sure to *communicate* your rates clearly to your clients and the fact that you expect payment in cash after completing the job. You may want to make a rate card for each of your clients' easy reference (and for yours, too!).

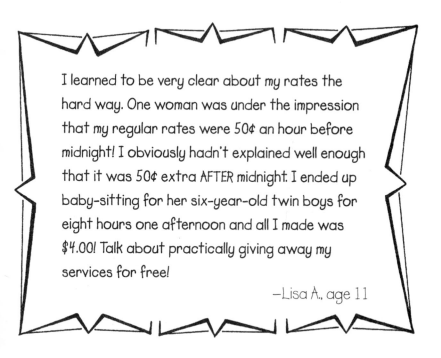

I learned to be very clear about my rates the hard way. One woman was under the impression that my regular rates were 50¢ an hour before midnight! I obviously hadn't explained well enough that it was 50¢ extra AFTER midnight. I ended up baby-sitting for her six-year-old twin boys for eight hours one afternoon and all I made was $4.00! Talk about practically giving away my services for free!

—Lisa A., age 11

If a potential client tells you that your rates are too high, don't get mad, or yell "later for you, Cheapo!" and hang up the phone. *Ask. Listen. Compromise.* If a client really cannot afford to pay the extra money after midnight, you may want to consider waiving the extra fee. Or let's say a client feels that your hourly rate is too expensive, you may want to consider reducing your rate by 25¢ or 50¢—it's all up to you.

LATER FOR YOU, CHEAPO!

When a client can't pay your designated fees, he or she runs the risk of your not being available to them for future jobs. You will most likely give first preference to the client who is able to pay your original, stated rates.

I really loved baby-sitting for the Eastmans— the kids were so well behaved, but the father always complained about how expensive *my* rates were. Eventually, all his comments started making me so uncomfortable that I stopped baby-sitting for them altogether. I hear that he has a lot of trouble finding good baby-sitters.

—Lexi D., age 15

Just remember: Don't undersell your-self either way! Money is important, but establishing and keeping good working relationships is just as important. Assess the situation. Are the chil-dren usually well-behaved?

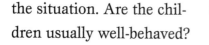

Are the children asleep most of the time, therefore giving you plenty of time to do your homework? Does this family have lots of good food and give you total munching freedom where the 'fridge is concerned? Figure out what your priorities are—believe it or not, it won't always be money.

Baby-sitter Beware

Money does strange things to people—it makes them act like they are from another planet. In other words, be prepared for any situation regarding money. Bring single dollar bills and

coins with you to a job just in case a client only has large bills and needs change.

There was this one family I used to baby-sit for that, at the end of the evening, would tell me that all they had was a $50 bill. The first time I had to wait till the next day to get paid because I didn't have change. The next time I brought change for a $50.00, and then they told me all they had was a $100 bill. Again, I had to wait to get paid. It was really frustrating. Eventually I stopped baby-sitting for them.

—Kara F., age 14

If a parent does not have enough money to pay after you have completed a job, tell him or her you can come by the next day to pick up your earnings. If, for some reason, a client does not pay you the next day, make sure to get the money before accepting the next job. It is OK to follow-up with phone calls until you get paid. If you have to leave a message, ask that the client get back to you within a reasonable amount of time. Most adults will not give you any trouble in this area.

Don't continue to work for someone who does not have money on hand or who always owes you money. This person not only doesn't have respect for themselves, they don't have respect for you. You are a baby-sitter, not the *tooth fairy* looking to give away your services for free.

⌒Meeting and Greeting

First conversations and impressions between you and your new client will most likely be over the telephone. Be friendly, be professional, and always be yourself. There's really no need to pretend that you're something you're not. Tell them how old you are, what your previous baby-sitting experience consists of, any relevant first-aid courses, and any other experiences you've had taking care of kids—even brothers and sisters. What you are trying to do is establish why you are a good choice for them as a baby-sitter. Be real. Be enthusiastic. Offer to send recommendations if you have any or give them phone numbers of responsible adults who can vouch for your character (make sure you first ask those adults if they would be willing to serve as references and accept phone calls from potential clients). Most potential clients just want to get to know you! Now, that's a cool concept—be yourself!

This is going to sound pretty weird, but one day after school, I picked up the phone using a phony British accent 'cause I thought it was going to be my friend on the other end. Anyway, it turned out to be a potential client! I was so embarrassed that I just couldn't bring myself to talk like my old New York self. Well, let's just say that the kids loved their "English nanny." I was totally relieved when this family got relocated to the midwest!

—Mike N., age 14

If you have an answering machine, keep your greeting brief and professional; loud music and laughing will scare off potential clients. Your best friend may think it's cute that you recorded your greeting with deep *burping* noises, but it's doubtful that a potential client will share your friend's warped sense of humor.

When hanging out at home, make sure to be always prepared when answering the phone. Keep your calendar and address book close by.

Here is a sample "Meet and Greet" phone conversation:

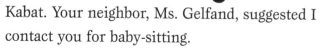

Potential Client: Hello, is Brian there?

Baby-sitter: Yes, this is Brian.

Potential Client: Hi. This is Mrs. Kabat. Your neighbor, Ms. Gelfand, suggested I contact you for baby-sitting.

Baby-sitter: Great, how nice of her. I baby-sit for Ms. Gelfand's son. How many kids do you have?

Potential Client: I have a son and a daughter.

Baby-sitter: And how old are they?

Potential Client: My daughter is three and my son is seven. Do you have experience with children these ages?

Baby-sitter: Oh, yes. I have a lot of experience with children of those ages. And, if you like, I can provide you with references. When did you need a baby-sitter?

Potential Client: I need a baby-sitter for this Saturday evening at 6:00.

Baby-sitter: Hold on, please. Let me check my calendar.

Saturday at 6:00 looks good. Approximately how many hours will you need me to baby-sit for?

Potential Client: My husband and I should be home around 11:00.

Baby-sitter: That's fine. I'm not sure whether Ms. Gelfand told you about my rates. My rates are . . . [now is the time to communicate to your potential client exactly what your rates are]. And I prefer to be paid the same day or evening in cash.

Potential Client: That sounds fair.

Baby-sitter: Let me take a moment to get from you the correct spelling of your name, address, and telephone number. Also, what are the names of your children?

Potential Client: My name is Madeline Kabat. K-A-B-A-T. Our address is 2671 Lucky Hollow Drive and the number is 555-1212. My children are Garett and Chloe.

Baby-sitter: I live only a few blocks away from Lucky Hollow Drive. I'll have no problem getting to you; however, will someone be able to drive me home in the evening?

Potential Client: Of course. That won't be a problem.

Baby-sitter: I usually like to arrive fifteen minutes early; however, since this will be the first time I am baby-sitting for you, would it be OK if I arrived a half hour earlier? That would give you enough time to show me around and explain all the rules of the house.

Potential Client: That sounds like a good idea. I'll see you on Saturday at 5:30.

Baby-sitter: Thank you. See you on Saturday.

Always make sure to figure out your means of transportation at the time of accepting a job—especially if you don't have a driver's license.

This first conversation was pretty simple, probably because you were recommended to the potential client by a neighbor. Someone who gets your name from a flyer may ask you many more questions. Be prepared with a complete answer for each question asked. Some questions could be:

☐ How old are you?

☐ How many years have you been baby-sitting?

☐ Do you have experience with infants and toddlers?

☐ Do you have any references? Would you please provide me with their names and telephone numbers?

☐ Are you familiar with basic first aid?

☐ Do you know CPR?

You may want to suggest to a potential client that you come over one afternoon for about 15–30 minutes so the two of you can meet in person before deciding whether or not you want to work together. This time

spent is a good investment in many ways. It will put both you and the potential client at ease. And even if you do not end up baby-sitting for this client, she or he will be sure to remember your professionalism and recommend you to friends. During this time, remember that not only is this person checking you out, but you are checking them out as well.

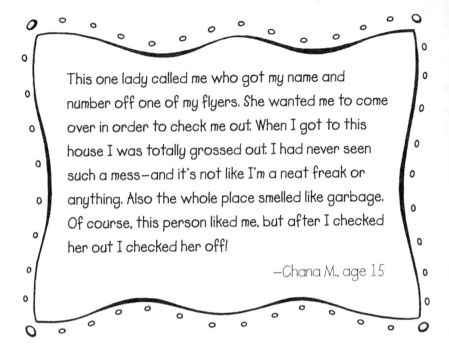

This one lady called me who got my name and number off one of my flyers. She wanted me to come over in order to check me out. When I got to this house I was totally grossed out. I had never seen such a mess—and it's not like I'm a neat freak or anything. Also the whole place smelled like garbage. Of course, this person liked me, but after I checked her out I checked her off!

—Chana M., age 15

Always remember that you don't have to take *every* baby-sitting job that comes your way. If you get a *weird* feeling (any kind of strange or uncomfortable feeling) from any potential clients, decline the job. Be smart and trust your instincts.

You may suggest to a potential client that the first time you baby-sit for his or her child can be while he or she is at home. This will help everyone get to know one another a lot better. Be prepared, however. Many KTWs (Kids to Watch), especially the younger ones, want to be with their parents or guardians if they know they are very close by. Don't take it personally. Try to distract the KTWs as best as possible.

References

References must be provided upon request. What exactly is a reference? A reference is someone who knows you either personally and/or professionally and is able to speak positively about you. Don't assume someone will be your reference, ask first. Ask someone you already baby-sit for, a neighbor who has seen you interact with children, your priest, minister, rabbi, or even a teacher who knows you well. It's a good idea to have a least three people whose names and numbers you can give to potential clients as references. Keep their names and numbers close by so that when a potential client calls, you don't have to dig for the numbers in your T-shirt drawer. If a reference chooses not to give out his or her phone number, you can ask for a signed, written recommendation. If someone doesn't want to be your

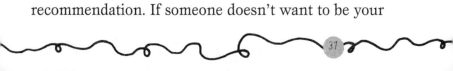

reference don't take it personally and don't egg their house the following Halloween—even though it may be very tempting.

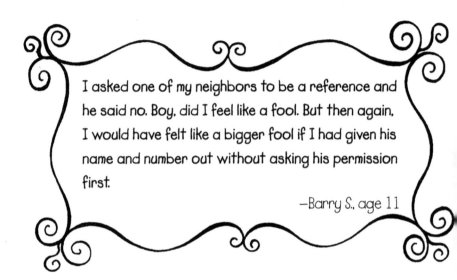

I asked one of my neighbors to be a reference and he said no. Boy, did I feel like a fool. But then again, I would have felt like a bigger fool if I had given his name and number out without asking his permission first.

—Barry S., age 11

CHAPTER 2

GETTING YOUR ACT TOGETHER

As horrible and difficult as it may be, getting organized is very important. The more prepared you are from the home base the more prepared you will be out in the field. OK, baby-sitting isn't *really* like going to war, but for some people it can sure feel like it.

Using a calendar is not only useful for keeping track of appointments and baby-sitting jobs, it will help you make sure you have enough time for everything else you want to do.

You might also want to jot down the birthdays of your KTWs to help you remember them on their special day with a card or a phone call.

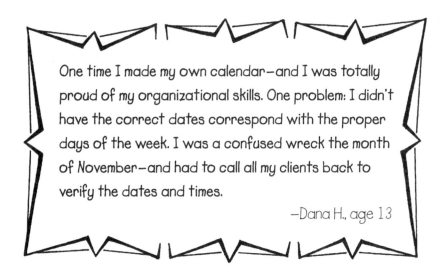

One time I made my own calendar—and I was totally proud of my organizational skills. One problem: I didn't have the correct dates correspond with the proper days of the week. I was a confused wreck the month of November—and had to call all my clients back to verify the dates and times.

—Dana H., age 13

Getting the Gang at Home Organized

The telephone number you give out will either be your own private number or your family's number. If you share a phone with your family, make sure to keep message pads and pens by all of the phones in your home. Ask all your family members to take messages for you—both names and telephone numbers. Try to call clients back the same evening, but don't call past 8:00 P.M. If it's past 8:00 P.M., call the very next day.

Getting Yourself Organized

You are a young *entrepreneur* now. Or rather, a young executive. Either way you say it—you are a business person waiting for the bucks to begin rolling in. Set up a calendar of events for each month. Write down holidays, after-school activities, baby-sitting appointments, mid-terms, finals, and days you won't be available to work. This will help you schedule all your appointments at a quick glance. If you have an important exam you need to study for, you probably don't want to schedule any baby-sitting appointments for the night before.

Don't ever assume you will be able to get a lot of studying done while baby-sitting. A baby who usually sleeps the entire time could suddenly wake up and be fussy for the rest of the evening. You'll get frustrated because you'll be thinking about the studying that needs to be done and you might not give the baby the appropriate attention. Remember, when you accept a baby-sitting job, your first priority is the KTW—the kid you are watching.

FEBRUARY

SUN.	MON.	TUES.	WED.	THURS.	FRI.	SAT.
					Baby-sit @the Fords' 6:45 P.M.	Shopping w Lisa Baby-sit @the Singers' 7:00 P.M. **1**
Skating with Jenn 12:30 P.M. **2**	Choir Practice 3:00 P.M. Baby-sit @the Roths' 6:30 P.M. **3**	Book Report Due **4**	Student council meeting 3:30 P.M. **5**	Gina's B-day **6**	Date with Scott ♡♡♡ **7**	Baby-sit @ the Singers' 6:30 P.M. **8**
Baby-sit @ the Bunchoos' 2:00 P.M.- 6:00 P.M. Movie @ Lisa's 7:00 P.M. **9**	Choir Practice 3:00 P.M. **10**	**11**	**12**	Baby-sit @the Fords' 6:00 P.M. sharp! **13**	VALENTINE'S DAY ♡ Date with Scott **14**	Baby-sit/assist @ b-day party for Jordan 10:30 A.M. 2:00 P.M. Jenny's party 8:00 Bring present **15**
BBQ at Scott's house 12:30 P.M. Baby-sit @ the Speregens' 5:00 P.M. **16**	Biology Quiz (No problem!) Choir Practice 5:00 P.M. **17**	**☀☀History presentation in one week Baby-sit at the Singers' 6:00 P.M. **18**	Study for Algebra mid-term! **19**	Algebra mid-term **20**	Date with Scott ♡♡ **21**	Shopping with "the gang" **☀Update calendar for next couple of months **22**
Mom's B-day (spend day with family) **23**	Choir Practice 3:00 P.M. **24**	History presentation (today!!) **25**	Student council meeting 3:30 P.M. **26**	**☀☀ Update baby-sitting card file **27**	**28**	MARCH Baby-sit @the Singers' 7:00 P.M. **1**

42

Baby-sitting Clubs

It all started with one great idea. Baby-sitting clubs have been the total rage for the past few years. And why not? Who better to go into business with than your friends? For *most* people, going into business with their friends is a good and fun idea.

Working for yourself has its advantages, such as being your own boss and getting to keep all the profits (otherwise known as money). But along with the advantages come disadvantages, such as having only yourself to rely upon.

About two years ago, my three best friends and I started our very own baby-sitting club. We put our money together and made up T-shirts with our club telephone number on the back of it. We went everywhere together wearing those shirts and got tons of business. Now we have seven members in our club because we couldn't handle all the business among just the three of us anymore.

—Cali A., age 16

BABY-SITTING CLUB RULES

✳ **BE** SUPPORTIVE OF ALL CLUB MEMBERS

✳ **MEET** ONCE A WEEK ON MONDAY FROM 3-4:30 AT LAURA'S HOUSE

✳ **ALL** DUES ARE TO BE COLLECTED THE FIRST MONDAY OF EVERY MONTH

✳ **NEW** CLUB OFFICERS ARE ELECTED EVERY SIX MONTHS

✳ **NO** SECRETS

_____
Baby-sitter's Signature

_____
Baby-sitter's Signature

_____
Baby-sitter's Signature

_____
Baby-sitter's Signature

Baby-sitting clubs have many of the same advantages as working for a company. A baby-sitting club can have as few as two members; howev-er, the club will prob-

ably work best with at least three members. Just remem-ber: The more members in the club, the more organiza-tion it will take since three (or more) schedules are hard-er to juggle than one.

The basic concept behind a baby-sitting club is to elect one person who will be in charge of all calls, a sort of operator whom all clients can call to schedule a baby-sit-ter. The baby-sitting club member with his or her own phone and answering machine would be the most logical choice for this job. This person will have everyone's schedule on hand and will book all the appointments. The person who takes on this job should consider the fact that there is extra work involved—especially since once you give clients one number to call for all of you, it may be a pain to later change your mind about who the main scheduling person is and to have to let all your clients know this. Some clubs pay this elected phone per-son 50¢ from each of their baby-sitting jobs as a fee for taking care of the club schedule.

You and the other club members can elect officers and set up a guideline of rules. You may want to consider charging monthly dues which can be used toward making and distributing flyers, buying munchies, throwing parties, or even planning special events just for you and the other club members.

Clients can request a specific baby-sitter; however, if this baby-sitter is unavailable, there will usually be another baby-sitter available. Another good thing about a baby-sitter's club is that you will always have a back-up to cover the clients on the list you have worked so hard to build. Let's say you accept a job on one particular evening, but something suddenly comes up. Well, you can always ask another member of the club to fill in for you. This will put your mind at ease as well as your client's. (But if a client has asked specifically for you, make sure he or she is notified in advance of any changes made. No parent or guardian likes surprises where their children's care is concerned.)

You and the other club members can pick a specific day and time when you all meet. Let your clients know that this is the time to call to set up appointments.

While you're all gathered together, review the rules, bring

up various club and baby-sitting issues, share ideas, and brainstorm on how to increase business. This is also a *fun* and *profitable* excuse to hang out with your friends and chow down on your favorite snacks.

Cherise and I formed a baby-sitting club together about three years ago. We are both co-presidents. Now we have eight members including two guys our age, which is just perfect. Last year we put our dues together and spent the day at Disneyland—without our KTWs. We had the best time ever!

—Alanna T., age 15

Baby-sitting clubs are definitely cool and very in. But know yourself. If you don't think you would work well with your friends or have time for weekly meetings, then perhaps a baby-sitter's club just isn't for you. It won't mean that you'll be less of an effective baby-sitter. It just means you want to do this solo, and that's more than OK. Many baby-sitters do just fine on their own, too.

Be Prepared

The word is out, the phones are ringing, and you are scheduling appointments! H-E-L-P!

Not to worry, you have it all under control. Make sure to keep handy your calendar of appointments and all the important information for a baby-sitting job. Attach to the back of your calendar a small piece of paper or index card with all the information you need for a particular job. The information should include the date you are baby-sitting, whom you are baby-sitting for, the time you are baby-sitting, the rate you are charging (this is very important if you are not charging your usual rate), the names of the KTWs, and the client's phone number.

So I spent this whole weekend getting everyone in the club organized and insisted on creating the master calendar which I promised to copy for everyone the next day. I made our calendar for the next six months, and then I lost it. It must have run away with the sock from the dryer. At first I was too embarrassed to call the clients back. But after one of the club members missed an appointment and we lost a very angry client, I had to call all of the clients and ask them all to tell me when we were scheduled to baby-sit at their homes. Boy, did I feel irresponsible.

—Jay B., age 14

Kid Watching Cards

Don't expect to remember everything—especially if you
have a lot of clients! The easiest way to keep track of
your KTWs is by making a *KTW Card*. These cards will
be for your own personal reference—or for the club's

DATE OF BABY-SITTING JOB: February 3
BABY-SITTING FOR: Wesley Singer
TIME: 7:00 P.M. – 1:00 A.M.
RATE: the usual
ADDRESS & PHONE NUMBER:
3709 Crest Road West
555-5555

Get to the Singers' by 6:45 P.M.
They will give me a ride home at night.

reference. Include the kid's name, what he or she likes or
doesn't like to do, any allergies, birthday, favorite books,
and any other information you think is important to
remember. Since kids grow and change so quickly, you
may want to update these cards every few months. So
when you are getting ready to baby-sit for the Hoffmeier
twins, Zachary and Dustin, you'll just whip out their

KTW card. Oh yeah, you almost forgot, they love it when you read them *Green Eggs and Ham*—for some crazy reason it calms them down right before bed time. Who would think that Dr. Seuss would have a calming effect instead of a hyper effect on the kids? You grab your personal copy off the bookshelf in your bedroom, stuff it into your backpack, and off you go to face the terror twins. Now you're armed and ready with ammunition—*Green Eggs and Ham*. Good thing you made a note of it on the KTW card.

UPDATED: JUNE 11

JORDAN NEWBERGER

BIRTHDAY: July 26, 1994

LOVES ♡ Chocolate and the book "Green Eggs and Ham"

HATES taking a bath and will sometimes cry when his parents first leave the house

LIKES to play with his trucks and likes when we dance silly.

Really FUN to play with.

Usually WAKES UP crying from his nap.

Making a Good Impression

It's probably a good idea for you to call and confirm a baby-sitting job with a new client a day or two before-hand. Also confirm a job if it was made a few weeks ahead of time. You don't want to arrive the day or evening scheduled to discover that a client's plans have changed and they forgot to call you!

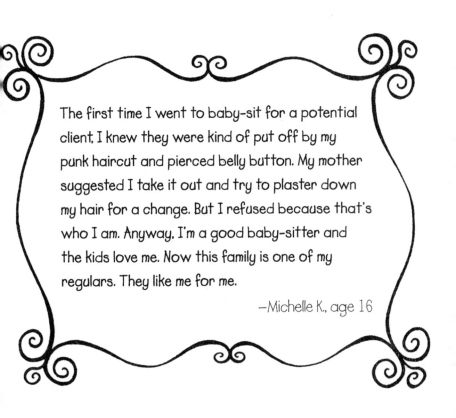

The first time I went to baby-sit for a potential client, I knew they were kind of put off by my punk haircut and pierced belly button. My mother suggested I take it out and try to plaster down my hair for a change. But I refused because that's who I am. Anyway, I'm a good baby-sitter and the kids love me. Now this family is one of my regulars. They like me for me.

—Michelle K., age 16

Arriving on Time

There are many ways to give clients the wrong impression. Arriving late is one way. If your clients can't depend on you to arrive on time, they won't feel as if they can depend on you to care for their children. Give yourself enough time to shower, dress, and pack up your stuff. If, for some reason, you are running late, make sure to call your client. Don't make a habit of it either.

Dressing the Part

Most importantly, dress comfortably. Of course that doesn't mean arriving in your pajamas or ripped *Hootie and the Blowfish* T-shirt. You still need to look neat, clean, and professional. Wear something that you don't mind getting dirty. Baby-sitting in your funky new shirt is not a good idea. As you know, kids can be rather messy.

I was supposed to baby-sit for my regular KTW, Troy, for only a couple of hours, and then go to my best friend's party. Since Troy was going to be asleep I decided to wear the outfit that I was also going to wear to the party. Of course, Troy woke up crying, and when I picked him up he vomited formula down the back of my shirt. I didn't have time to go home and change, so after taking care of Troy I cleaned my shirt as best as possible. The whole night at the party people kept crinkling up their noses around me and asking whether I smelled something weird. I was so humiliated.

—Laurie P., age 12

The little boy or girl you baby-sit may have a major crush on you, but that doesn't mean you have to dress up for him. Dress for success—and in this case it means dress comfortably. I'm convinced that leggings and sweat pants were designed with baby-sitters in mind.

CHAPTER 3

SAFE AND SOUND

As you have heard many times before, your safety truly is number one. This doesn't mean that you should get all paranoid that something bad will happen. It just means that you should be prepared for everything.

DON'T EVER WALK HOME ALONE—EVER!

There and Back

Make sure you know how you're getting to and from a baby-sitting job. If you have a driver's license, make sure you have enough gas to get you to the job and back home again. Have your client watch you or walk with you to your car at night. Take the main streets home or make sure to drive along well-lit streets. Keep all doors in your car locked. If you don't drive, make all transportation arrangements before accepting a job. Are you bicycling, getting a ride from a trusted adult, or getting picked up by the client? At night, will your client drive you home? *Don't* ever walk home alone at night. Even if you live just down the block, make sure your client drives or walks you home.

Let Someone Know

Make sure your mom, dad, or someone else with whom you live knows the name, address, and phone number of where you will be baby-sitting. Also, let them know the approximate time when you expect to be home. Make it part of your baby-sitting routine to jot down this information, and keep it by the phone or on the refrigerator in your home.

June 12

Mom,
   I'm baby-sitting
for the Conns from 3:30
till about 7:00 P.M. They
live at 333 Fourteenth
Street. (555-5555)
   See ya later!
       Deb

Trust Your Instincts

Driving While Under the Influence

Your personal safety is very important. If a parent comes home *intoxicated* make sure not to get into a car with him or her. An intoxicated person is someone who is drunk or on some other drug. Intoxicated people can act many different ways: loud, aggressive, unable to stand or walk straight, and slurring their words. Be polite but firm with the intoxicated person. *Don't* worry about insulting the client. Call your own parent or guardian (no matter what time), and ask for a ride home. You and your parents or guardians should have already had a discussion that, in the event you call for a ride, they will pick you up without question and you will explain the situation later. If your parents or guardians are not at home, then call a taxi. Keep the number of a local taxicab company handy so that if a situation like this should arise, you don't have to start flipping through the phone book at that moment. If you don't have enough money for a taxi, then call the parents or guardians of your bestfriend. *Never* go home alone from a night job. Your safety is number one.

> Mr. and Mrs. Smith came home totally wasted—
> they smelled like rubbing alcohol and beer. It was
> completely gross. I was feeling kind of nervous, but
> I stayed calm. Mr. Smith wanted to drive me home,
> but I told him that I had already made arrangements
> for my dad to pick me up. He was so drunk that he
> couldn't even tell I had just made that up. I called
> my dad and, no questions asked at that moment, he
> came immediately. My folks won't let me baby-sit
> for the Smiths anymore.
>
> —Carla A., age 12

Inappropriate Behavior

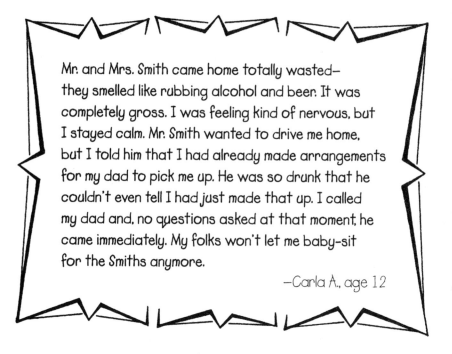

What do you do if a parent *comes on* to you? In other words, if he or she makes a sexual advance or pass at you? A parent's actions may not be obvious. What if a client puts a hand on your knee, tells you a sexy joke, or uses foul language in your presence? Once again, *trust your*

instincts. Trusting your instincts means listening to the little voice in your head that is getting the signal from the pit in your stomach which says, "Hey, something feels very weird and uncomfortable, and I can't quite put my finger on it." You may ask a client to stop by simply saying, "Mr. X, I don't like it when you say things like that around me. Please don't." There is no need to get into a long discussion about what exactly is making you feel uncomfortable. If an uncomfortable situation continues, leave and *don't* baby-sit for that family anymore.

Child Abuse

Child abuse is a *very serious* accusation. Child abuse can be either physical, emotional, or both. There are *many* signs of abuse and these are just a few of them: An abused child *could* act very cranky, reclusive, timid, aggressive, or scared when you raise your hand in even the most gentle manner, or be unwilling to change his or her clothes in your presence for fear you will notice bruises. An abused child might even tell you something fishy or perhaps you might notice that every other time you come to baby-sit, the child has a new limb in a new cast.

Professionals who are trained in child safety have enough difficulty detecting abuse, so just imagine how hard it would be for you to determine whether or not one of your KTWs is actually being abused; however, if you feel you have a legitimate reason and evidence that leads you to seriously suspect child abuse, speak to your parents or guardians or any other trusted adult in your life. Let this trusted adult know exactly what you have observed, and why you think abuse is taking place. He or she will probably be able to provide you with good advice. Or, you may want to speak to a family doctor, priest, or rabbi. They, too, should be able to guide you as to how to best handle this situation.

~ Safety First

As a baby-sitter, you are responsible for not only your own safety, but also for the safety of your KTWs. Take your job very seriously.

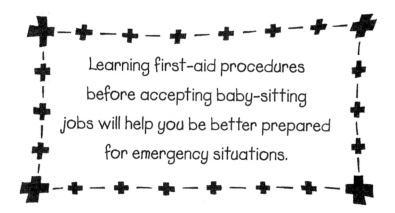

Learning first-aid procedures before accepting baby-sitting jobs will help you be better prepared for emergency situations.

Look into whether your local YMCA, American Red Cross, or community center offers baby-sitting safety classes or first-aid classes. These classes will definitely be worth your time to take. Not only will the knowledge you gain put your mind at ease, but it will also give your clients more confidence in your baby-sitting abilities.

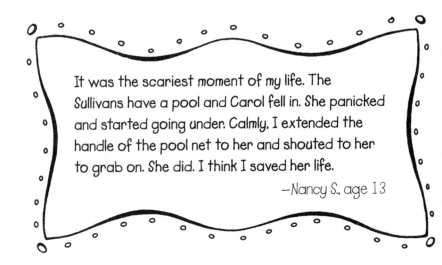

It was the scariest moment of my life. The Sullivans have a pool and Carol fell in. She panicked and started going under. Calmly, I extended the handle of the pool net to her and shouted to her to grab on. She did. I think I saved her life.

—Nancy S., age 13

BABY-SITTER CHECKLIST:

☐ Keep handy the name, address, and phone number of where you are baby-sitting.

☐ Know the nearest major and minor cross streets to the street where you are baby-sitting.

☐ Know the location and phone number of where your clients can be reached in case of an emergency.

☐ Know the name and number of an alternate person or neighbor to contact in an emergency if the parents or guardians of your KTWs cannot be reached.

☐ Keep emergency numbers, a pen, and pad of paper near the telephone.

☐ Make sure you know the locations and instructions on the use of safety equipment such as fire extinguishers and first-aid supplies.

☐ Walk through the house with the parents or guardians to ensure all doors and windows are locked before they leave.

☐ In the evening, make sure the outside lights are on.

BABY-SITTER "DO NOT" CHECKLIST:

☐ **DO NOT** allow strangers into the house unless the parents specifically inform you to let them in.

☐ **DO NOT** tell a caller that you are a baby-sitter alone with the children. Take a message and let him or her know the call will be returned shortly.

☐ **DO NOT** go outside to investigate suspicious noises or activities. Turn on the outside lights and call the police.

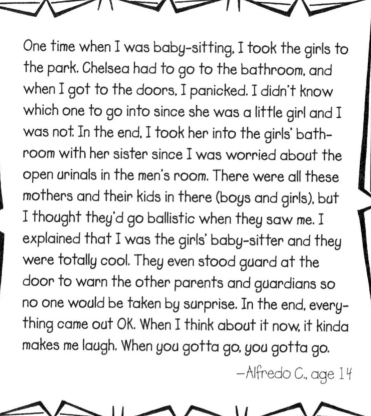

One time when I was baby-sitting, I took the girls to the park. Chelsea had to go to the bathroom, and when I got to the doors, I panicked. I didn't know which one to go into since she was a little girl and I was not. In the end, I took her into the girls' bathroom with her sister since I was worried about the open urinals in the men's room. There were all these mothers and their kids in there (boys and girls), but I thought they'd go ballistic when they saw me. I explained that I was the girls' baby-sitter and they were totally cool. They even stood guard at the door to warn the other parents and guardians so no one would be taken by surprise. In the end, everything came out OK. When I think about it now, it kinda makes me laugh. When you gotta go, you gotta go.

—Alfredo C., age 14

ON-THE-JOB SAFETY CHECKLIST:

☐ Before the parents or guardians leave, ask for
all the information on the *Baby-sitter Checklist.*
Keep this list near the phone at all times.

☐ Ask the parents or guardians to show you the
location of emergency exits, smoke detectors,
and fire extinguishers.

☐ Make sure you have the telephone number and
address of where the parents or guardians will
be. Ask whom is authorized to grant medical
permission in an emergency situation if parents
or guardians can't be reached. Write down that
person's phone number.

☐ If the house or apartment has an electronic
security system (burglar alarm), learn to use it
and get all necessary codes or secret passwords
to give to the police in case the alarm goes off by
accident.

☐ Be sure you know how to lock and unlock the
doors and windows, especially if a key is need-
ed. Lock all doors and windows and leave outside lights on.

☐ Do not open the door to strangers. Don't let anyone at the door or on the phone know you're there alone. If asked, respond by saying that you are visiting, the children's parent or guardian cannot come to the phone or door, and you will deliver a message.

☐ When the KTWs go to sleep, make sure to check on them regularly. Every fifteen minutes is appropriate for babies and toddlers, every thirty minutes is fine for older children.

☐ Stay awake while baby-sitting.

☐ If you are baby-sitting during the day and you take the KTWs in the back yard, make sure the front door is locked and vice versa. But don't lock yourself out. And *never* leave a child unattended or out of eyesight while they are awake, even for a second!

☐ If you ever feel uneasy or suspicious about something you hear, don't hesitate to call the police.

If you plan on taking the KTWs to a park or anywhere else, make sure to have a key which locks and unlocks the doors of the house or apartment. Double-check doors and windows before you leave.

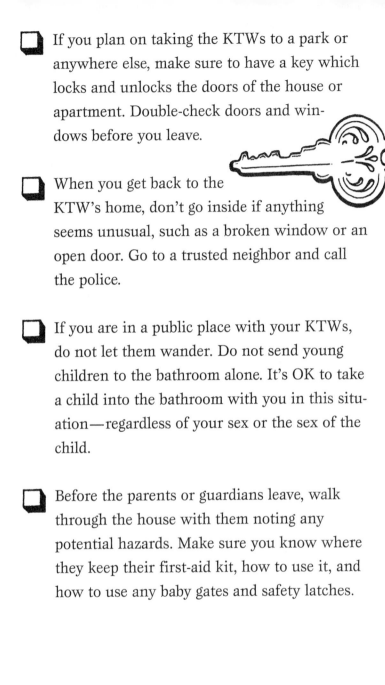

When you get back to the KTW's home, don't go inside if anything seems unusual, such as a broken window or an open door. Go to a trusted neighbor and call the police.

If you are in a public place with your KTWs, do not let them wander. Do not send young children to the bathroom alone. It's OK to take a child into the bathroom with you in this situation—regardless of your sex or the sex of the child.

Before the parents or guardians leave, walk through the house with them noting any potential hazards. Make sure you know where they keep their first-aid kit, how to use it, and how to use any baby gates and safety latches.

One time when I was baby-sitting I heard this really strange noise coming from the parents' bedroom downstairs while I was upstairs. All the KTWs were asleep, and so I thought it would take too long to wake them up and run over to a neighbor's place. So I called 9-1-1. The police came right over. It turned out that the neighbor's Husky jumped in through an open window and was sniffing around the bedroom. I was really embarrassed, but the police and the parents told me that I had done the right thing. Now I always check to make sure that all the windows are closed and locked before the parents leave for the evening.

—Helene B., age 13

In an Emergency

Emergencies are situations that could be potentially dangerous and require immediate action. Emergencies are also problems you are not expected to handle all alone. You *are* expected, however, to call for help. Most areas use 9-1-1 as the official emergency number. Check your local telephone directory for the Emergency Medical Service number in your area. If the number is not 9-1-1, then write down the correct number, and put the piece of paper somewhere safe. Memorizing this emergency number would be a great benefit, too.

When you call 9-1-1, be calm and let the operator know that you are the baby-sitter. Try to answer all the emergency operator's questions to the best of your ability. Listen carefully to all of the instructions you are given by the emergency operator. Be prepared to provide the emergency operator with the following information:

- ❑ the address and phone number of the home you are at

- ❑ the type of emergency

- ❑ the child's age

- ❑ your name and the KTW's family's name

Try not to panic during an emergency. It will not only hinder your ability to think clearly, it will also frighten the KTWs.

Fire

If there is a fire, quickly get the KTWs and yourself **OUT**! Go to a neighbor's and call 9-1-1 or the fire department. If you can, call the parents from a neighbor's and let them know where you and the KTWs are, and what is happening.

Poison

If you suspect that one of the KTWs has swallowed poison, contact 9-1-1 immediately or the Poison Control Center (the number is in the front of the telephone book and should be on your list of emergency numbers) or the family physician. Try to be able to identify the suspected poison and the amount taken. If you cannot find the Poison Control Center number, then don't waste precious time looking for it. Dial 9-1-1 or the Emergency Medical Service number in your area.

Bleeding

Try to stop excessive bleeding by applying pressure directly to the wound. Use a clean piece of cloth, bed sheet, bath towel, or cloth diaper to help stop the bleeding. Use wads of paper towel or a shirt if nothing else is available. *Do not* apply pressure if the child's eye or ear is bleeding. As soon as you can, call 9-1-1.

Drowning

If you don't know how to swim, make sure to let your clients know—especially if they have a pool or expect you to take the KTWs swimming. If you've taken a life-saving course, then use your knowledge and skills to rescue your KTW. If you do not have trained lifesaving skills, do anything you can to get the KTW out of the water; extend an object so he or she can grab onto it such as a towel, a long heavy stick, or even a tennis racquet. As soon as the child is pulled to safety, phone for help. If you do not know how to swim and the water is deep, do not jump in after the KTW. This will endanger not only the KTW's life, but yours as well. Yell for help.

Broken Bones

Tell the KTW to stay where he or she is and do not move. Call 9-1-1 immediately and return to the KTW while you wait for help to arrive. Try to immobilize the broken bone with something straight and stiff like a board, so as to not cause further damage.

For severe falls, burns, electric shock, or unconsciousness call 9-1-1 immediately.

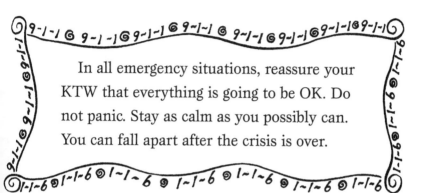

In all emergency situations, reassure your KTW that everything is going to be OK. Do not panic. Stay as calm as you possibly can. You can fall apart after the crisis is over.

CHAPTER 4

ASKING ALL THE RIGHT QUESTIONS

The KTWs have said goodbye to their parents or guardians. Now you're in charge! Think of the possibilities—the freedom, the power—but where do you draw the line?

Pigging Out

Most clients are pretty cool about letting the baby-sitter eat on the job. It's best, however, to check with the parents or guardians as to what food is OK and not OK for you to eat. The last thing you want to do is eat your clients out of house and home. Can you imagine not being called back to baby-sit because you made an absolute pig of yourself? Oink, oink.

Also, find out whether they mind your using the oven or not. If using the oven is OK, be careful. Stay in the kitchen while something is cooking, and make sure to turn off the stove and oven when you are finished. Keep children away from these hot and potentially dangerous surfaces. Basically, use common sense when cooking.

I admit it. I was a total idiot. My clients came home to find me sitting down to a meal I had just microwaved for myself: Pork chops and applesauce. The father was really angry—it was supposed to be his dinner that evening. I had thought it was just leftovers. I suggested they deduct it from my rate, but they didn't. They just never called me again.

—Peter B., age 14

Find out whether the KTWs have any food allergies. You don't want to bring a child one of your famous fudge brownies with walnuts that you specially baked, only to learn that he or she is allergic to nuts (this is the type of information you would then add to your KTW Card).

Feeding Babies

Make sure the parents or guardians instruct you what, when, and how to feed the baby. If you have never sterilized a bottle, or mixed formula, or burped a baby, make sure to ask the parents to show you how to do it properly. It's OK not to know everything. It's not OK to pretend that you do. The best way to heat a bottle is by putting the base of the bottle in a large glass of very hot water. Keep the nipple away from the hot liquid—you don't want to burn your KTW's lips. If you heat up a bottle, shake out some of the milk onto your forearm to test the temperature. The milk should be neither hot nor cold, but lukewarm.

Keep a cloth diaper or clean towel nearby. Babies are very messy eaters. Don't be alarmed if a baby spits up more of his or her milk than he drinks—this is normal. (However, spitting up is different from violently and repeatedly throwing up. If this happens, call 9-1-1 immediately.) After feeding and burping the baby, make sure to clean the baby, yourself, and the kitchen.

Thinking about tasting the baby's formula? Think again. That is unless the thought of spoiled, milky chalk sounds tempting to you!

Feeding Toddlers

Prepare a toddler's meal *before* placing him or her in the high chair. A squirming toddler in an unattended high chair is an accident in the making. After

you've prepared the meal, then put the toddler in the high chair making sure he's securely strapped in. Children this age like to feed themselves, so don't get too concerned if the food lands in more places than the mouth. You'll have plenty of time to clean up. If the toddler doesn't want to eat a lot, don't be too concerned. Just make sure to mention it to the parents or guardians when they return home.

If the floor below the high chair is difficult to clean or might get stained, place a towel underneath the chair to catch any splatters.

Some toddlers *hate* to have their faces wiped clean. Wet a cloth with warm water and make a game of cleaning by asking questions such as, "Where's your nose?" Then wipe the smudge off his or her nose.

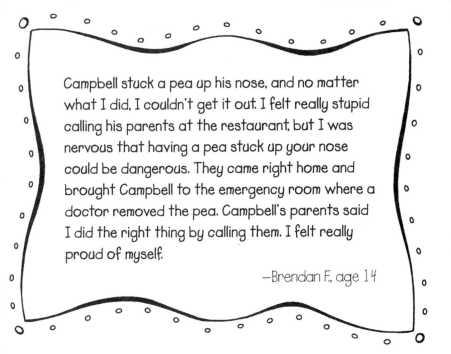

Campbell stuck a pea up his nose, and no matter what I did, I couldn't get it out. I felt really stupid calling his parents at the restaurant, but I was nervous that having a pea stuck up your nose could be dangerous. They came right home and brought Campbell to the emergency room where a doctor removed the pea. Campbell's parents said I did the right thing by calling them. I felt really proud of myself.

—Brendan F., age 14

Feeding Young Kids

Eating with young kids can be fun, frustrating, and at times, totally disgusting. Many kids will test your patience by asking for many different things to eat at once. Hold your ground but be flexible. Remember, you are the boss in charge of this situation. Never lose your cool and always keep your sense of humor. Who knows, you might find you really do love pickles smeared with peanut butter.

A favorite game for young kids is "see food." You'll get a great view of dinner from the tongue's perspective.

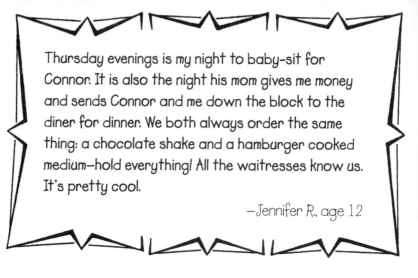

Thursday evenings is my night to baby-sit for Connor. It is also the night his mom gives me money and sends Connor and me down the block to the diner for dinner. We both always order the same thing: a chocolate shake and a hamburger cooked medium—hold everything! All the waitresses know us. It's pretty cool.

—Jennifer R., age 12

WE'LL HAVE THE REGULAR!

If parents don't give you detailed instructions on what to serve, make foods that are easy to prepare, delicious to eat, and easy to clean up. Most kids like to eat peanut butter and jelly sandwiches (they make a healthy breakfast), cereal (yes, even for dinner), funky-cut fruit-salad, spaghetti, pizza, and grilled cheese sandwiches.

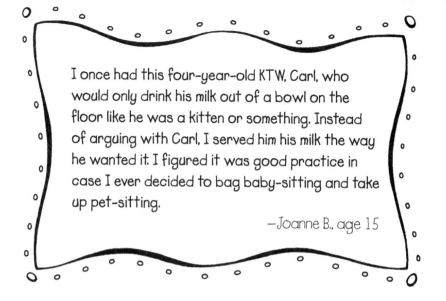

I once had this four-year-old KTW, Carl, who would only drink his milk out of a bowl on the floor like he was a kitten or something. Instead of arguing with Carl, I served him his milk the way he wanted it. I figured it was good practice in case I ever decided to bag baby-sitting and take up pet-sitting.

—Joanne B., age 15

Chowing down is very fun, but just remember that you are baby-sitting not attending a food tasting contest. If you have no self-control (like I don't), try eating before going to a client's house or bring your own snacks.

Rules of the House

You may think it's OK for a child to read in bed until he or she falls asleep no matter how late it is; however, the family you are baby-sitting for may not think the same way. Get all the rules of the house before deciding things on your own.

☐ **Bed Time.** Find out what time to put the kids to bed. Ask whether or not they are allowed to read before lights out. What types of books are they allowed to read? How late are they allowed to stay awake reading?

☐ **Homework Time.** Ask whether the child has any homework and, if so, how much time you should give them to do it. (Is it OK to offer your assistance to the KTW during homework time?)

☐ **Videos, Video Games, Computer, and TV Time.** Ask whether it's OK for the KTWs to play video games, use the computer, or watch TV for as long as

they would like. Some parents restrict this to only an hour and only after all the homework has been done.

■ **Phone Time.** Is it OK for the older KTWs to talk on the phone? If yes, for how long? Ask whether there is call waiting. You wouldn't want a KTW (or you for that matter) tying up the phone line for hours at a time.

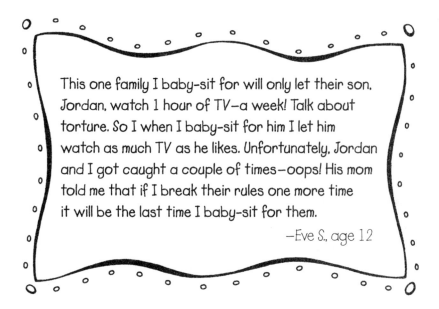

This one family I baby-sit for will only let their son, Jordan, watch 1 hour of TV—a week! Talk about torture. So I when I baby-sit for him I let him watch as much TV as he likes. Unfortunately, Jordan and I got caught a couple of times—oops! His mom told me that if I break their rules one more time it will be the last time I baby-sit for them.

—Eve S., age 12

OK, we all know it: People can be rather weird about their home and their rules. Ever wonder why people are so uptight? Yeah, me too. If only people would loosen up a bit and not take themselves so seriously. Now, that's my rule—but it applies only in my own home where I am boss. I would never try to make up rules for other people. Always respect a client's house and child-caring rules.

"Where's My Bear?" and Other Issues

Ask the parents or guardians whether there are any special duties or instructions they have for you. Most parents will appreciate your asking since they are probably in a rush to get out of the house and have too much to remember as it is. Don't be embarrassed to write down any special instructions. You, too, have a lot to remember. You may also want to add some of these special instructions to your KTW Cards.

A special instruction could be something as important as what kind of medication to give a child and at what time, to which stuffed animal a baby likes to fall asleep with. You may think the latter is silly—but if you ever try to get a child to fall asleep without his or her favorite thing, you might think again!

Find out whether the parents would like you to give the KTW a bath before putting him or her to sleep for the night. If you have never given a young child a bath, and prefer not to, then let the parent know this before arriving at the job. If you do feel comfortable giving a child a bath remember to:

☐ Check the temperature of the water before the child gets into the tub.

☐ *Never*, even for a second, leave the baby or child unattended; if the phone rings, let it ring.

☐ Keep a firm grip on a baby or young child when they are in or near the bath water.

☐ Don't fill the tub too high with water, four to eight inches is plenty.

Instead of giving a bath to a baby or young child, you may feel more comfortable giving him or her a warm sponge bath outside of the tub, using a clean, wet washcloth.

Time for Bed

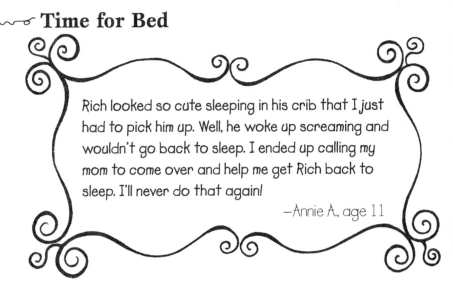

Rich looked so cute sleeping in his crib that I just had to pick him up. Well, he woke up screaming and wouldn't go back to sleep. I ended up calling my mom to come over and help me get Rich back to sleep. I'll never do that again!

—Annie A., age 11

Babies

When putting a baby to sleep, first make sure that he or she has a clean diaper on. You want the baby to fall asleep feeling dry and comfortable. Some babies cry when you put them down to sleep. Always lay a baby on his or her back and not his or her stomach. Try gently rubbing his or her back and softly singing a song. These two actions may soothe the child. Then tiptoe out of the room. Let the baby cry for two minutes or so and then go back in the room and start soothing all over again. Never let a baby cry for more than three minutes. After a while the baby will fall asleep. Always be patient with babies and young children.

Toddlers and Young Children

Most kids don't like going to sleep, especially when they are having such a good time with you, the best baby-sitter on earth! Putting your KTWs down for the night can be a very positive experience. First of all, prepare the KTW early that bed time is approaching. Give them plenty of advance warning, starting at 15 minutes, then 10, then five. If you're in the middle of playing a game or watching television let them know how much longer before it's time to go to bed.

"Rachel, it's 7:15 now. I'll be tucking you in bed in fifteen minutes."

"Rachel, it's 7:25 now. Five more minutes and it's time for dreamland."

"OK, Rachel, let's pick out a book together, and I'll read it to you when you're under the covers."

KTWs will try to bargain with you. Hold your ground. Be firm, but be gentle. Make going to bed a very special experience between you and your KTW. Read a bedtime story or make up your own story.

Dream Box

A dream box is something that young children or even older children will like. Take a shoebox and decorate the outside with very soothing colors, clouds, stars, or anything else you think the child will like. Then on little pieces of paper, write down nice things that a child can dream about. When the child is in bed, have him or her close her eyes, reach into the Dream Box, and pick out a piece of paper. Have her open it up and read aloud what she will dream about tonight. With very young children you may have to read it to them. Then put the piece of paper underneath their pillows.

Be creative with the dreams you write down. A few examples might be:

☐ Dream about being in a candy store and being allowed to taste anything you want.

☐ Dream about your next birthday party.

☐ Dream about being a famous ballerina, sports star, superhero, or superheroine.

☐ Dream about being at the amusement park with your best friend.

☐ Dream about the tallest ice-cream sundae ever made.

☐ Dream about finding a famous pirate's treasure chest.

You know how you don't like to leave a party early or go to sleep when your best friend is staying over? Well, it's sort of the same thing for your KTW when you are there. He or she doesn't want to miss any of the action, either. No need to explain that all he or she is missing is your studying for some algebra exam. Just be patient.

CHAPTER 5

KTW DO'S AND DON'TS

One of the most rewarding aspects of baby-sitting is having fun! Playing with children can and should be a wonderful experience. Of course, kids will be kids and you are the responsible grown person in any baby-sitting situation. After making sure your games are both safe and age appropriate, hop, wiggle, crawl, dance—be as silly as your KTW!

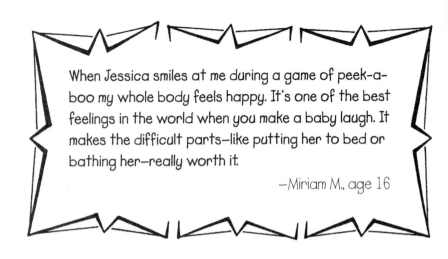

When Jessica smiles at me during a game of peek-a-boo my whole body feels happy. It's one of the best feelings in the world when you make a baby laugh. It makes the difficult parts—like putting her to bed or bathing her—really worth it.

—Miriam M., age 16

∿ Babies

Baby Do's

Babies love bright colors, objects that jingle such as keys and bells, and funny noises. Peek-a-boo and other games of "now you see it, now you don't" are sure to make them giggle. They like to be held, gently bounced, sung to, and danced around with. Even if you don't know any baby songs ("Old Mac Donald Had a Farm" will do), make up one. It's not necessarily the words that babies are entertained with, but rather it's the tone of your voice and the expressions on your face. Help them to dance or clap by laying them in your lap and moving their hands or feet to the music. Go to the library and check out a book of nursery rhymes or watch a kids' song video for some ideas. Check out some of the Wee Sing® books and cassettes at your local book or music store!

Baby Don'ts

Never leave a baby unattended. If you have to go to the bathroom and can't take the baby with you, put the baby safely in the playpen or crib. Never give a baby a small object that can be swallowed. All objects should be the same size or bigger than his or her fist. If a baby won't stop crying and you've tried everything from feeding him or her to changing the diaper then try rocking him or her or pacing back and forth cuddling the child in your arms.

Toddlers

Toddler Do's

Toddlers like to sing, dance, be tickled, and be read to. They also like scribbling on a piece of paper with crayons and watching  videos. Toddlers also like puppets. An easy way to make a puppet is to take an old white sock and draw a funny face and design on it with colored markers. Give the sock puppet a name, and bring it along with you to entertain your toddler KTWs. Pretend the puppet is talking in a strange language and use different voices and sounds. Don't worry about feeling silly—your KTWs will have a blast!

Toddler Don'ts

Before you can count to two, your toddler KTW will be into everything—and I mean everything!—and making a mess! Toddlers seem to have specially honed radar for electrical outlets, steep staircases, plastic bags, the pointy end of tables, fireplaces, cleaning supplies, and just about everything that they should *not* be near. So watch your toddler KTW very carefully. Also, children this age like to say the word, "No." Even when they mean yes, they still say no. So don't go getting crazy, it's just a phase (believe it or not, you went through it, too!).

Young Children

Young Children Do's

Children older than toddlers like to draw, make crafts, build forts, play by themselves, watch television, and play games with their baby-sitter. Ask your KTW what he or she would like to do. If he or she doesn't know what to do, then it's up to you to suggest something fun. Suggest playing a board game, a game of cards, or hide and seek. You could play beauty parlor or barbershop—get ready for a new you courtesy of your KTWs! (In chapter seven, we'll talk about more activities.)

Young Children Don'ts

Even though these kids are older, they still need to be looked after. So if your older KTW wants to play alone in his or her room that's fine; however, don't let him or her lock the door to the room. You always want to have easy access to all rooms in case of an emergency. And, every half an hour, don't forget to pop your head into the room to check that everything is OK. If the door is closed, knock before entering. Respecting your KTW is as important as your KTW respecting you.

✂ "But Mom Lets Me Do It"

This is something kids say a lot to the baby-sitter. Just because mom lets Max hang upside-down from the staircase banister, doesn't mean you have to. Use your judgment, and always consider the child's safety. Let Max know that you'll ask his parent whether this is OK, and if the parent says it is, perhaps next time you'll let him act like a monkey. Don't debate the issue. Quickly suggest another game or activity that's just as fun.

✂ Sibling Rivalry

Guess what? You are not only a baby-sitter, you are also a referee! And, just like a referee, you must remain neutral during all arguments. Scott says that Mark hit him first, but Mark claims that Scott hit him first. It doesn't matter. You were not around to witness the argument and, even if you were, you don't want to take sides. Let the siblings know that they must play separately for a while until they both feel they are able to play together

without arguing or hitting. Help each child find something constructive to do.

Yikes! There is so much to remember what to do and what not to do with babies and kids. Keep a cool head on your shoulders. Remember, if your parents were able to handle it, so can you.

CHAPTER 6

BABY-SITTER DO'S AND DON'TS

Even when a parent tells you to "make yourself right at home," you may do so—but remember that there are limitations. No matter how comfortable you are at your KTWs' house, you must still be respectful and follow the rules of *their* home. When in doubt as to what you should do, proceed with caution.

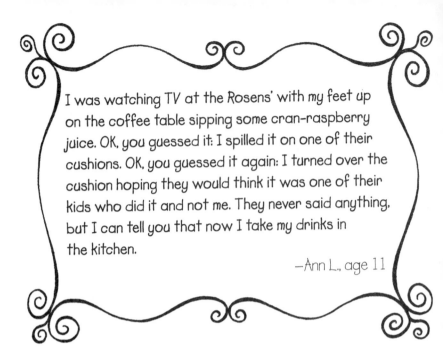

I was watching TV at the Rosens' with my feet up on the coffee table sipping some cran-raspberry juice. OK, you guessed it: I spilled it on one of their cushions. OK, you guessed it again: I turned over the cushion hoping they would think it was one of their kids who did it and not me. They never said anything, but I can tell you that now I take my drinks in the kitchen.

—Ann L., age 11

"Rrrringg"

Phone Messages

Answer the phone politely. And don't forget, never tell the caller on the other end that you are a baby-sitter alone with the children. It is better to be overly cautious. Take clear messages. Get the correct spelling and phone number of the person who is calling. Also jot down the time that the person called. Leave the message by the phone. When the parents or guardians come home, let them know that there is a phone message and where you left the message. You may want to bring along a small pad of paper and pencil just in case you can't find one in the home at which you're baby-sitting.

Checking In

Most clients call at some point to check in to make sure that everything and everyone is OK. If it is, then assure the client that everything is fine. Even if it took you two hours to get the baby to fall sleep, but he is finally sound asleep, then assure the clients that the baby is sleeping. Save the details for when they come home. If anything serious happened in their absence and you were unable to contact them, however, do not wait until later to inform them—even if everything is fine by the time they call. I can assure you that they will *not* appreciate your trying to protect them from unpleasant news about their precious children.

Using the Phone

OK, so your best friend just went out on this incredible date with the cutest guy in your class. The KTWs are safely tucked in bed, hopefully sleeping like angels. This does not give you the license to sit on the phone for hours at a stretch. And if you do have permission to use the phone, make sure the family you are baby-sitting for has call waiting. You don't want the parents or guardians or one of their friends continually listening to a busy signal. And, unless it's extremely urgent, do not make long distance phone calls. Make sure to ask the parents or guardians if it's OK for you to make a local phone call to a friend in the area.

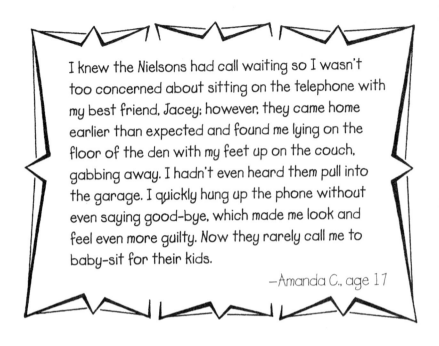

I knew the Nielsons had call waiting so I wasn't too concerned about sitting on the telephone with my best friend, Jacey; however, they came home earlier than expected and found me lying on the floor of the den with my feet up on the couch, gabbing away. I hadn't even heard them pull into the garage. I quickly hung up the phone without even saying good-bye, which made me look and feel even more guilty. Now they rarely call me to baby-sit for their kids.

—Amanda C., age 17

Food

One of the other fun aspects about baby-sitting is snacking at someone else's house. Make sure to ask whether or not you may help yourself to some of the food. If the answer is yes, make sure not to eat someone out of house and home, and don't assume yes means helping yourself to the T-bone steak

in the freezer or the last chocolate chip cookie in the cupboard. Use your good judgment. Most importantly, whether you make something for yourself or for one of your KTWs, clean up the mess! The last thing a parent or guardian wants to come home to is a messy kitchen or crumbs all over the house.

I just love baby-sitting for the Hartwicks. Not only are the kids a ton of fun, but they have the best food. They have all kinds of ice-cream, chips, and cookies. It's like baby-sitting in a supermarket.

—Paul F., age 14

Friends

Baby-sitting can sometimes get a bit lonely, especially after the KTWs have gone to bed. You may want to have your good friend come baby-sitting with you. Before you do invite someone to come along, make sure to get permission first. Make it very clear to the parents or guardians that the person you would like to have along with you is reliable and trustworthy. Assure the clients you understand and are fully aware that even though you have a friend along that first and foremost your responsibility is to their children. Also assure the parents that there will be no extra charge for the extra helping hand.

∿ **Keeping Awake**

Once the KTWs have gone to bed, you, the baby-sitter, are going to want some things to keep you entertained while awaiting the clients' return.

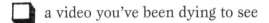

HOMEWORK

A VIDEO YOU'VE BEEN DYING TO SEE

KNITTING OR ANY OTHER HOBBY THAT YOU DO THAT IS PORTABLE

NOW IS A GOOD TIME TO UPDATE YOUR KTW CALENDAR

A GOOD BOOK

MAGAZINES

STATIONERY FOR CATCHING UP ON LETTER WRITING

☐ homework

☐ a video you've been dying to see

☐ knitting or any other hobby that you do that is portable

☐ now is a good time to update your KTW card files

- [ ] a good book

- [ ] magazines

- [ ] stationery for catching up on letter writing

Snoozing

No matter how difficult it may be to avoid, don't fall asleep! You are not used to waking up to the sounds of a crying baby and may run the risk of sleeping through the calls of a small child or even an emergency situation. If you know that you can't stay up past a certain hour, then don't accept baby-sitting jobs where you know you will be out very late.

If you do feel yourself getting sleepy try:

- [ ] jumping jacks

- [ ] running in place

- [ ] sitting up in an uncomfortable chair

- [ ] sipping a cold drink

- [ ] watching a funny movie

Team Sitting

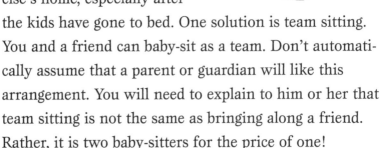

Does the baby-sitter, you, need a baby-sitter? Some people don't like being all alone or don't feel comfortable in someone else's home, especially after the kids have gone to bed. One solution is team sitting. You and a friend can baby-sit as a team. Don't automatically assume that a parent or guardian will like this arrangement. You will need to explain to him or her that team sitting is not the same as bringing along a friend. Rather, it is two baby-sitters for the price of one!

Pros of team sitting:

❑ You have company to help keep you from feeling lonely, scared, and from falling asleep.

❑ Four responsible eyes and hands are better than two.

Cons of team sitting:

❑ Not all parents will like this idea of having two baby-sitters in their home at the same time.

❑ You may have to split all the earnings.

You may only want to team sit in the evenings when you may feel more uncomfortable by yourself in the house with sleeping KTWs.

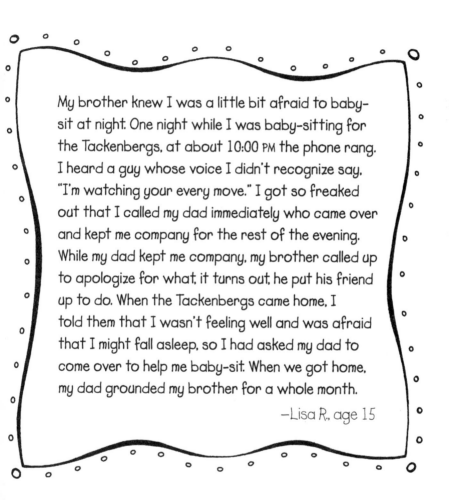

My brother knew I was a little bit afraid to baby-sit at night. One night while I was baby-sitting for the Tackenbergs, at about 10:00 PM the phone rang. I heard a guy whose voice I didn't recognize say, "I'm watching your every move." I got so freaked out that I called my dad immediately who came over and kept me company for the rest of the evening. While my dad kept me company, my brother called up to apologize for what, it turns out, he put his friend up to do. When the Tackenbergs came home, I told them that I wasn't feeling well and was afraid that I might fall asleep, so I had asked my dad to come over to help me baby-sit. When we got home, my dad grounded my brother for a whole month.

—Lisa R., age 15

Cold Chills Down Your Back

Once the kids have been safely tucked in bed for the night the last thing you want to do is freak yourself out! It's amazing that when the KTWs were up, you didn't notice the house creaking or the wind blowing outside. Suddenly every noise sounds like someone is right outside waiting to get in. First of all, stay calm and don't panic. Remind yourself that all the doors and windows are securely locked. If it will make you feel better, check the locks one more time. Then make sure not to do certain things that will totally scare yourself to death.

☐ Don't watch any scary movies, watch a comedy.

☐ Don't watch the news or real crime shows, watch reruns of your favorite TV show or music video.

☐ Don't sit in a dark room, sit in a well-lit room.

CHAPTER 7

PLAY TIME!

There are so many different games and ways to entertain your KTWs. Most children love the most simple games and the ones that require lots of imagination.

Games Galore

Look around your own room, attic, or basement for games and toys from your childhood. If they're not in bad condition, bring them to that certain KTW. Just remember, don't begin playing a long board game like Monopoly™ or Life™ right before bedtime.

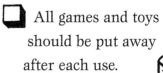 All games and toys should be put away after each use.

 Make cleanup time a fun part of play time.

If you can, try not to take out too many toys at once. First of all, it will make it more difficult for a KTW to concentrate on one particular toy or game. Second, it will make cleanup time a lot more difficult for you.

Activity Box

Create an activity box which you bring along to all your baby-sitting jobs. In this box keep small toys, games, and some basic art supplies. Update the contents of this box every month. Some toys and games you can include in the activity box are: a small rubber ball and jacks, colored markers, a yo-yo, a kazoo, some scraps of old material or felt, yarn, some old socks, glue, kiddy scissors, and anything else you think of that is fun.

Check out your local 99¢ store or nearby garage sales for some other cool items to put in your activity box. Also, check out a storybook each month from the library and keep it in the activity box. The KTWs will be excited to see what new book their baby-sitter has brought along to share.

Sock Toss

To play Sock Toss, gather a laundry basket, a plastic bowl, some clean rags, and three pairs of rolled up socks. Make sure to roll up the socks and secure them with rubber bands.

Put the small bowl into the basket and line the inside of the basket with rags. Next, make a throw line for the kids to stand behind. Tossing the sock into the basket is worth one point while making it into the bowl is worth three points. Start off by playing 10 rounds. After everyone has had an equal number of turns, add up the scores. The person with the highest score wins!

Tongue Twisters

KTWs of all ages just love tongue twisters. And this is something that will keep them amused while you are in the kitchen preparing a meal or cleaning up after a meal. Go to your local library and get a book with all kinds of tongue twisters. Try these:

Frank threw Fred three free throws
or
Rubber baby buggy bumpers

Fingerprint Painting

This is a very fun and easy activity to do with your KTWs. All you need is tempera paint, heavy paper plates, paper, and colored markers.

Make sure to spread lots of newspaper or a plastic sheet on the floor and table before starting any arts and crafts projects.

Pour a small amount of paint onto a heavy paper plate. Have the KTWs press one, two, or even every finger into the paint and then onto a sheet of paper. Let the paint dry for a couple of minutes. Then, with the colored markers, have the KTWs add details to the finger prints and the background.

Books

Children love to read books and they love being read aloud to. Go to your local library and become familiar with storybooks and chapter books. If something catches your eye and amuses you, then perhaps it will also amuse one of your KTWs. Ask the librarian to recommend some books. Or glance through publications that recommend books for children such as *The New York Times Parents' Guide to the Best Books for Children.*

When reading aloud to children, speak clearly and slowly. Try speaking in different voices for each different character. The only rule to reading is to have fun!

Calming Down Your KTWs

When the KTWs get a little bit too wild for your liking, then it's time to calm them down and suggest some soothing activities. Try reading, popping in a video, or playing some soft music.

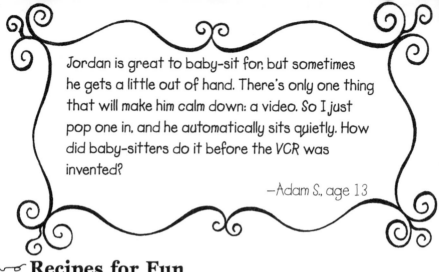

Jordan is great to baby-sit for, but sometimes he gets a little out of hand. There's only one thing that will make him calm down: a video. So I just pop one in, and he automatically sits quietly. How did baby-sitters do it before the VCR was invented?

—Adam S., age 13

Recipes for Fun

KTWs get the munchies. Satisfy their cravings by making caramel apples, popcorn balls, pretzels, and many more scrumptious snacks.

Remember, never let the KTWs operate the oven, stove, or sharp utensils. All cooking should be done under your supervision. This rule applies to all recipes and any activities involving sharp equipment, utensils, or hot electrical appliances.

FUDGY CARAMEL APPLES

Ingredients:

6 hard yummy apples

1 package (14 ounces)
    candy caramel cubes

2 tablespoons hot water

¼ cup chocolate chips

*You can use a microwave or a double boiler to melt the candy.

Microwave Instructions:

1. Wash and dry the apples.
2. Poke an ice cream stick into the stem end of each apple.
3. Pour caramels, hot water, and chocolate chips into a microwave-safe bowl and cover with a microwave-safe plate.
4. Microwave on high for two minutes. Stir.
5. Repeat until mixture has melted.
6. One at a time, dip apples into the mixture. Using a spatula, scoop mixture onto apples until they are covered.
7. Now put the apple, stick up, on the wax paper to cool and harden.

Double Boiler Instructions:

1. Put 1 inch of water in the bottom part of the double boiler.
2. Put candy mixture in the top part of the double boiler.
3. Melt mixture on medium, stirring occasionally. When mixture has melted, remove double boiler from heat, keeping top part over the hot water.
4. One at a time, dip apples into the mixture. Using a spatula, scoop mixture onto apples until they are covered.
5. Now put the apple, stick up, on the wax paper to cool and harden. *Snappy apples—delish!*

PERFECT POPCORN BALLS

Ingredients:

7 cups unsalted and
   popped popcorn
3 cups miniature marshmallows
2 tablespoons butter
$\frac{1}{4}$ teaspoon salt
food coloring (optional)
butter or cooking oil
*You can use a microwave or a double
boiler to melt the candy.

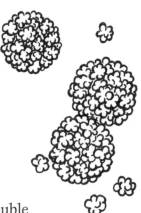

Microwave Instructions:

1. Put miniature marshmallows, butter, and salt into a
   microwave-safe bowl. Cover bowl with a microwave-
   safe plate.
2. Microwave on high for two minutes. Stir.
3. Repeat until mixture has melted.
4. Add a few drops of a wild shade of food coloring.
5. Pour popcorn into a bowl.
6. Pour melted marshmallow mixture over popcorn and
   stir gently to coat.
7. Lightly coat your hands with butter or cooking oil.
   When you are certain the mixture has cooled,
   scoop out handfuls, shape them into balls, and let
   them harden on wax paper.

Double Boiler Instructions:

1. Put 1 inch of water in the bottom part of the double boiler.
2. Put marshmallow mixture in the top part of the double boiler.
3. Melt mixture on medium, stirring occasionally. When mixture has melted, remove double boiler from heat and add a few drops of a wild shade of food coloring.
4. Pour popcorn into a bowl.
5. Pour melted marshmallow mixture over popcorn and stir gently to coat.
6. Lightly coat your hands with butter or cooking oil. When you are certain the mixture has cooled, scoop out handfuls, shape them into balls, and let them harden on wax paper. *Popety-popety-pop!*

HOT & YUMMY PRETZELS

Ingredients:

1 cup warm water

2 packages active dry yeast

2 tablespoons sugar

3 cups all-purpose flour

2 tablespoons butter or shortening

1 egg

coarse salt (kosher salt)

pastry brush

1. Pour the cup of very warm water into a large mixing bowl and add the yeast. Stir until the yeast is completely dissolved.

2. Add the sugar and stir. Gradually add the flour and keep stirring. As you are adding the last of the flour, the dough will become stiff and dry—this is how it should be.

3. Sprinkle some flour on the countertop or on a breadboard. Flour your hands. Now knead the dough for about five minutes by pressing it flat with the heels of your hands, folding the flattened dough in half, and then pressing it flat again.

4. Form the dough into a ball, put it back into the bowl, cover the bowl with a dish towel, and place the bowl in a warm, dark place for at least 30 minutes. The rising dough will just about double in size.

5. While the dough is rising, heat the oven to 400° F. Grease or butter a cookie sheet.

6. When the dough has risen, put it back on the floured breadboard or counter. Flour a rolling pin and roll out the dough into a square shape about one-fourth to one-half inch thick. Using the dull back of a table knife, cut the dough into strips about as wide as your fattest finger with a back and forth sawing motion. You don't have to be exact.

7. Form each strip into a pretzel shape and pinch the ends together. As you handle the long strips of dough,

try not to let them stretch too thin. Place the pretzel-shaped dough on the greased cookie sheet.

8. Beat the egg in a small bowl for a minute, and with a pastry brush, coat the top of each pretzel with the egg.

9. Now sprinkle the salt, to your liking, over the doughy pretzels.

10. Let pretzels rise in a warm place until they double in size. It should take about 25 minutes.

11. Bake the pretzels for about 12–15 minutes or until they are golden brown.

   Twist to your heart's content!

ANYTIME-OF-THE-DAY SHAKE

Ingredients:

1 cup buttermilk or ¾ cup plain
   low-fat yogurt and ¼ cup lowfat milk

1 cup of fresh fruit, cut up
   (banana, pineapple, strawberry,
   mango—the riper the better)

1 teaspoon sugar (optional)

½ teaspoon vanilla

3 ice cubes or ⅓ cup crushed ice

Place all the ingredients in a blender, and process until they are well combined and frothy.

Shake it up, baby!

DELICIOUS PITA PIZZAS

Ingredients:

2 round (9–10 inch) pita breads

1 cup pizza sauce or tomato sauce

1 cup shredded cheddar cheese

1 cup mozzarella cheese

$^3/_4$ cup chopped cooked vegetables
(broccoli, zucchini, eggplant, and/or peppers)

1 cup chopped cooked meat
(ham, turkey, chicken, salami, and/or sausage)

1. Preheat oven to 400°F. Split each pita bread into
2 thin rounds. Arrange rough-sides-up on
baking sheets.

2. Spread each pita with about 3 tablespoons of sauce
and sprinkle each with $^1/_2$ cup of each cheese.

3. Top with a sprinkling of vegetables and/or meat.

4. Bake 5–8 minutes, until pizza is hot and the cheese
is melted.

Mama mia, pizza pie!

HOLY MOLY MACARONI AND CHEESE

Ingredients:

$^1/_4$ to $^1/_2$ pound grated cheddar
and parmesan cheeses

salt

2 cups milk

2 tablespoons cornstarch

½ pound (2 cups) elbow macaroni

1. Boil a large pot of salted water to cook the pasta.
2. Whisk the milk and cornstarch together in a medium-sized saucepan and set aside.
3. Add the macaroni to the boiling water and cook until tender, about 10 minutes.
4. At the same time, slowly bring the milk and cornstarch to a simmer, whisking constantly over medium heat. As the milk comes to a simmer, it will thicken. Stir ¾ of the cheese into the sauce and reduce the heat to very low. Cook, stirring constantly, until the cheese melts. Add the remaining cheese, remove the pan from the heat, and let the remaining cheese melt.
5. Drain the water from the elbow macaroni and toss it in with the sauce.

Elbow macaroni? Who invented such a silly food?

GOING BANANAS

Ingredients:

4 bananas, not too ripe

½ cup brown sugar
    (packed)

1 tablespoon lime juice

sour cream (optional)

1. Preheat the broiler part of an oven.
2. Peel the bananas and slice into circles ½ inch thick.

3. Mix the brown sugar and lime juice and toss it with the banana slices.

4. Spread the bananas in a shallow baking pan and broil until the sugar has melted into a glaze—usually 3–5 minutes.

5. Serve immediately with sour cream.

    No monkeying around!

PEANUT BUTTER ROUNDS

Ingredients:

⅓ cup butter or
  margarine

½ cup peanut butter,
  smooth or chunky

½ cup dark-brown
  sugar (packed)

1 egg

½ teaspoon vanilla

1 ¼ cups white flour

¾ teaspoon baking soda

½ teaspoon nutmeg

2 tablespoons sesame seeds

1 egg white, lightly beaten

½ cup chopped walnuts or granola

1. In a medium bowl and with an electric mixer, beat the butter or margarine, peanut butter, brown sugar, egg, and vanilla until the mixture is light and fluffy.

2. Sift the flour, baking soda, and nutmeg into the peanut butter mixture. Add the sesame seeds, and stir the mixture until the ingredients are well combined.

3. With your hands, form 1-inch balls of dough. Dip each ball into the beaten egg white, and then roll it in the walnuts or granola. Place the balls on lightly greased cookie sheets about 1–2 inches apart.

4. Bake the rounds in preheated 375°F oven for 10 to 12 minutes. Remove them from oven and let cool before eating. *Licky sticky yummy!*

CRUNCHY HOMEMADE TORTILLA CHIPS

Ingredients:

1 package corn or flour tortillas
2 tablespoons oil
pastry brush

1. With a pastry brush, paint a very light coating of oil on one side of each tortilla.

2. With a sharp knife cut each tortilla in half, then into quarters, then into eighths.

3. Arrange the pieces greased side up on lightly oiled baking sheets. Toast the chips in a preheated 350°F oven for about 10 minutes or until they are crisp and just beginning to brown.
¡Olé!

SPICY (OR NOT) SALSA DIP

Ingredients:

2 medium tomatoes, finely chopped

$\frac{1}{2}$ cup chopped scallions

2 tablespoons very finely chopped hot
  pepper (either canned or fresh green
  chilies or jalapeno pepper—careful
  to make sure you choose
  spiciness carefully—don't
  burn up the kids!)

1 tablespoon red wine vinegar

1 tablespoon oil

1. Combine all the
   ingredients in a small bowl.
2. Chill the dip for 30 minutes or longer.
3. Serve with homemade tortilla chips.

   ¡Ay caramba!

CHAPTER 8

OTHER WAYS TO MAKE MONEY

There are many ways to make extra money other than baby-sitting. The following jobs can be approached in the same manner as baby-sitting in terms of finding clients, making flyers, and scheduling appointments. The skills you've acquired in learning to baby-sit will give you a head start in becoming a success at many other jobs.

Pet-Sitting

Many people don't like to leave their pets at a kennel over a long period of time. Why not pet-sit? Pet-sitting can entail anything from visiting the pet a couple of times a day to feed, play with, or walk the animal, (depending upon what it is) or just once a day to feed it (like fish). Charge per visit to the home or for the entire period of time if the family is on vacation.

Dog-Walking

Many people must get a very early start in the morning and often come home very late at night. Why not offer your services as a dog-walker? Charge an hourly rate and guarantee at least one hour of fun and exercise for the dog.

For pet-sitting and dog-walking, introduce yourself to the local breeders, pet shop owners, and groomers. Let the owners know that you are in the pet care business and ask to hang a flyer in a window or place a business card on a counter.

Elderly Care

Many elderly people are lonely and welcome the opportunity for some company. Offer your services as a companion. A companion might be expected to go shopping and walking with their elderly friend. You may want to offer your services to do some light cleanup either in the house or outside in the yard.

Home Sitting

When the neighbors go away on vacations or business trips they often need someone to collect the mail and newspapers, care for the pets, and water the plants. You could be that person. This is also a service you can offer to your baby-sitting clients.

Party Assistant

Assist parents or guardians with their kids' parties (an extra pair of hands is always necessary). If you have special entertaining skills and can give a magic show or dress up like a clown and lead the kids in fun activities, suggest yourself as entertainment for the KTWs so the parents or guardians can relax a bit.

Car Washer

Do you have a hose, sponge, clean rags, car washing soap, and wax? Find an open spot that is near a water spout, make

signs, and you are in business! (Make sure to first get permission from whomever owns the location where you are setting up business.)

Gardening

Mowing the lawn, planting flowers, trimming dead leaves, and weeding is another service you can offer around the neighborhood. Also, consider raking leaves in the fall and shoveling snow in winter.

Homework Helper

Is there any subject you particularly excel in? Why not teach long division? Test a child on the multiplication tables. Conduct spelling drills. Assist a child who is having difficulty reading. As a homework helper, be prepared to validate your credibility by showing your report card to parents of potential clients as well as having recommendations from teachers and the school principal.

You can make this a fun time, too, by playing school. You're the teacher and the kids are the students! Lead the class in a different setting like under a tree, in a park, or any other fun place.

So there you have it! Everything you need to know about baby-sitting and making money. Don't forget about me, the author of this book, when you make your first million!